I0164839

Backyard
Bugs
& Creepy-
Crawlies

Mosquitoes

Ashley Lee

Explore other books at:
WWW.ENGAGEBOOKS.COM

VANCOUVER, B.C.

e WWW.ENGAGEBOOKS.COM

Mosquitoes: Level 1
Backyard Bugs & Creepy Crawlies
Lee, Ashley 1995 –
Text © 2022 Engage Books
Design © 2022 Engage Books

Edited by: A.R. Roumanis

Text set in Epilogue

FIRST EDITION / FIRST PRINTING

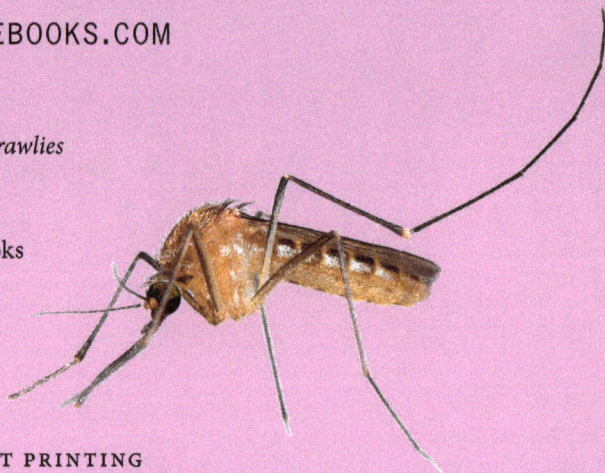

All rights reserved. No part of this book may be stored in
a retrieval system, reproduced or transmitted in any
form or by any other means without written permission
from the publisher or a licence from the Canadian
Copyright Licensing Agency. Critics and reviewers may quote
brief passages in connection with a review or critical article in any
media.

Every reasonable effort has been made to contact the copyright holders of all material
reproduced in this book.

LIBRARY AND ARCHIVES CANADA CATALOGUING IN PUBLICATION

Title: Mosquitoes / Ashley Lee.
Names: Lee, Ashley, author.
Description: Series statement: Backyard bugs & creepy-crawlies
Engaging readers: level 1, beginner.

Identifiers: Canadiana (print) 20250448542 | Canadiana (ebook) 20250448569
ISBN 978-1-77878-706-5 (hardcover)
ISBN 978-1-77878-715-7 (softcover)

Subjects:
LCSH: Mosquitoes—Juvenile literature.

Classification: LCC QL737.P94 C38 2025 | DDC J599.885—DC23

This project has been made possible in part
by the Government of Canada.

Canada

Contents

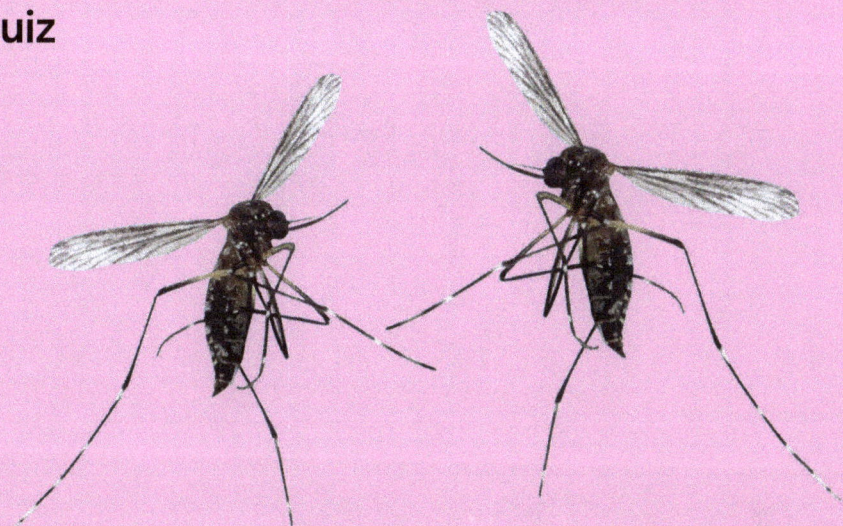

What Are Mosquitoes?

Mosquitoes are small flies. They were on Earth when dinosaurs lived.

Mosquitoes are one of the most common insects. There are more than 3,500 kinds of mosquitoes.

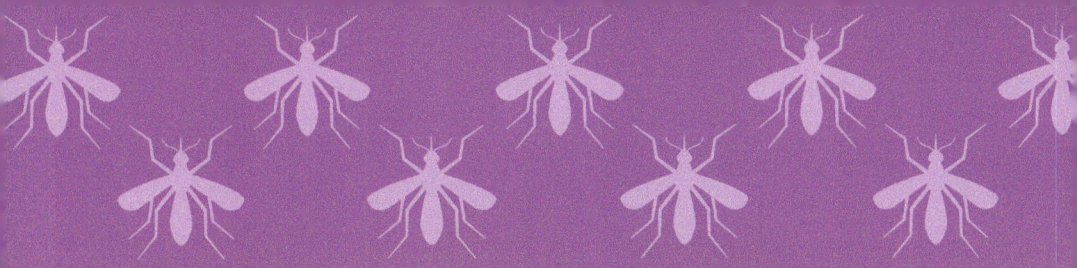

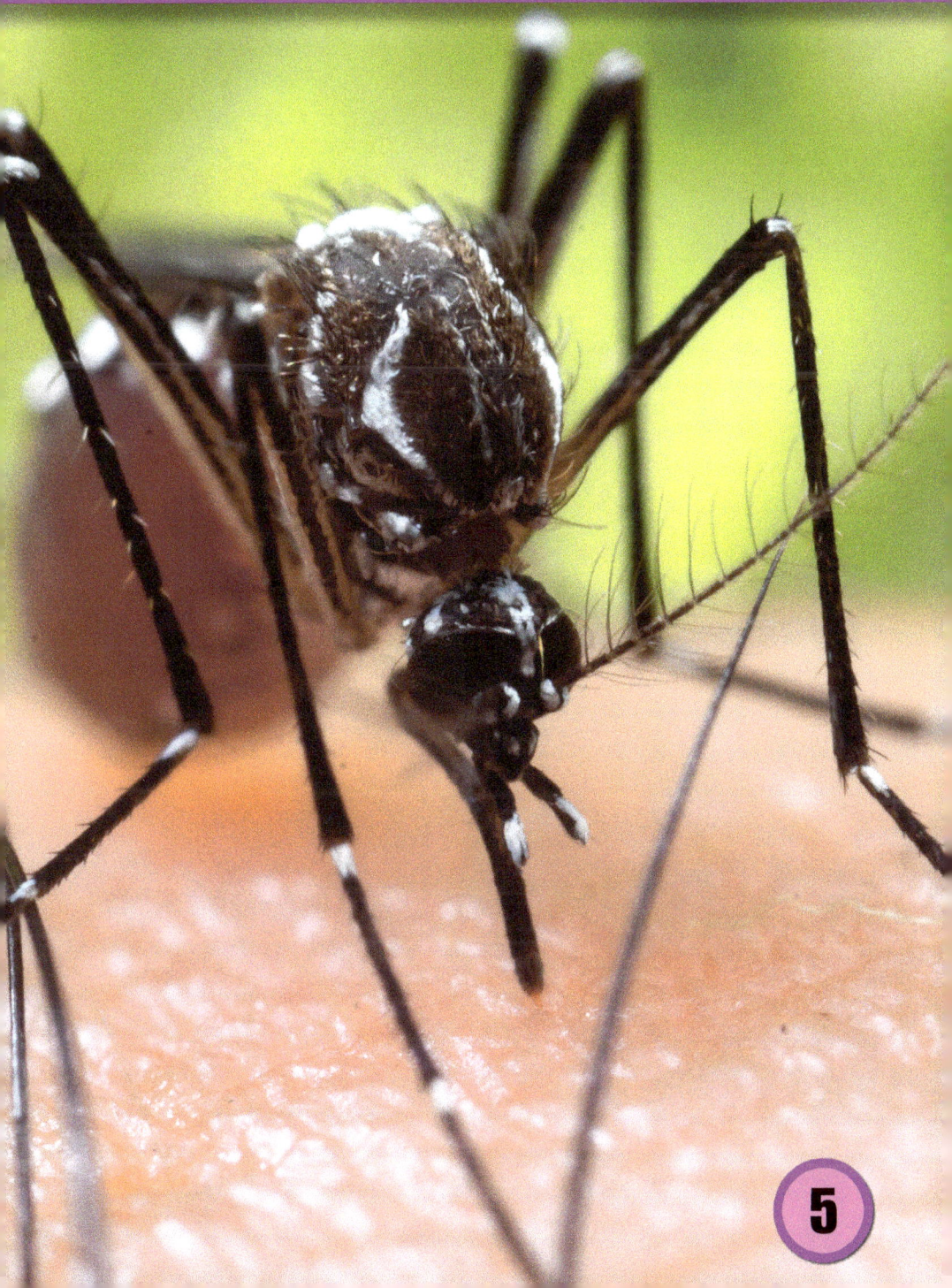

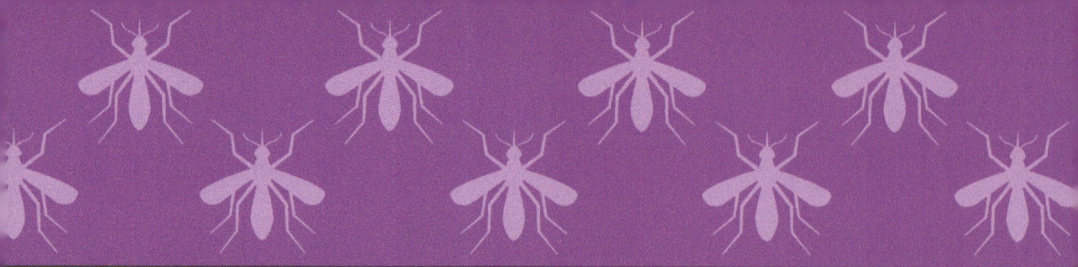

What Do Mosquitoes Look Like?

Mosquitoes have long feelers. Sometimes they look like feathers.

Feeler

Mosquitoes have six legs. Their back legs are longer than their front legs.

A mosquito mouth looks like a long tube. It is called a proboscis.

Mosquitoes have four wings. Only the front wings are used for flying.

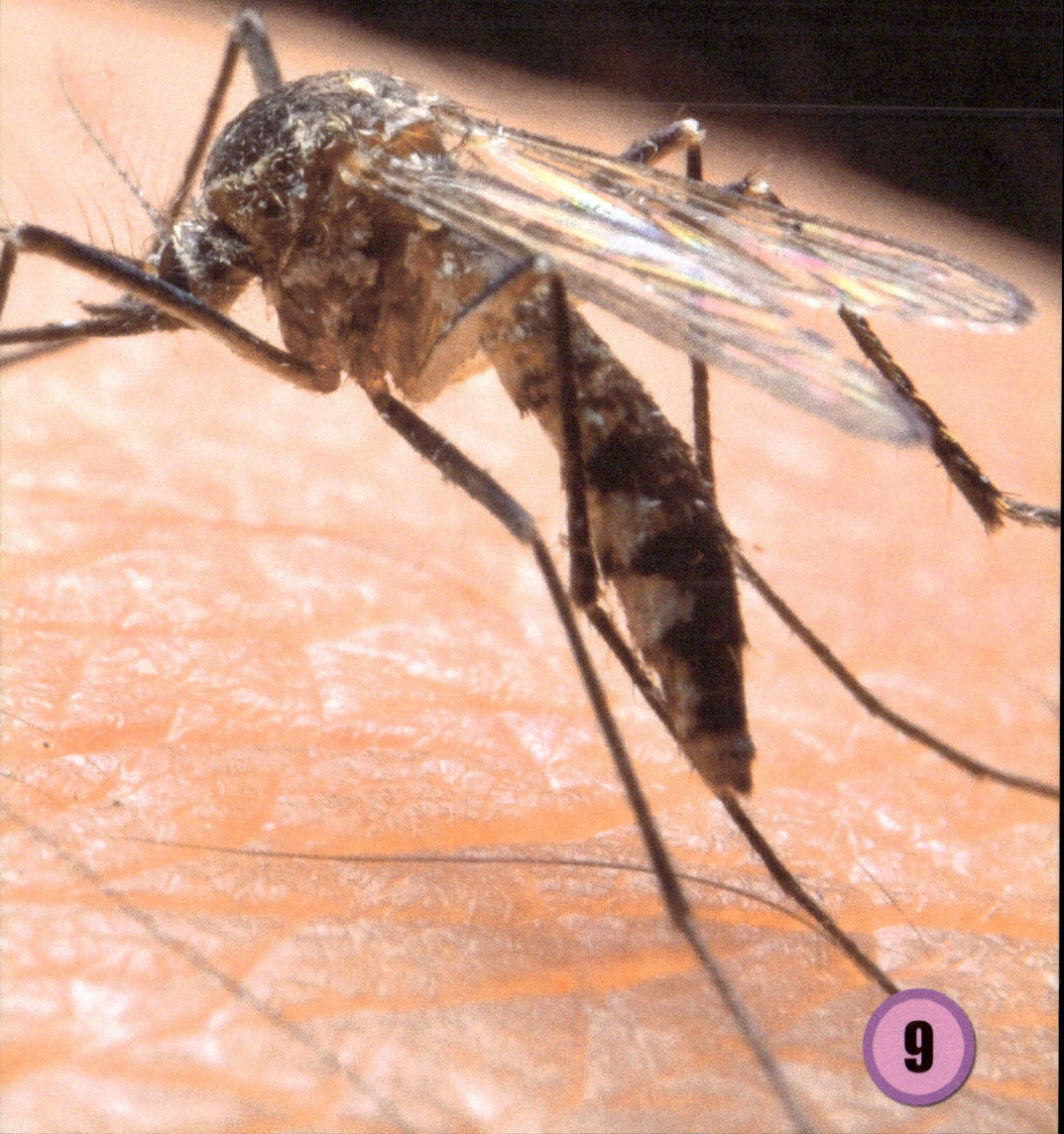

Where Do Mosquitoes Live?

Mosquitoes live all over the world. The only place they do not live is in Antarctica.

Some mosquitoes like to live near people. Others like to live in forests or grasslands.

10

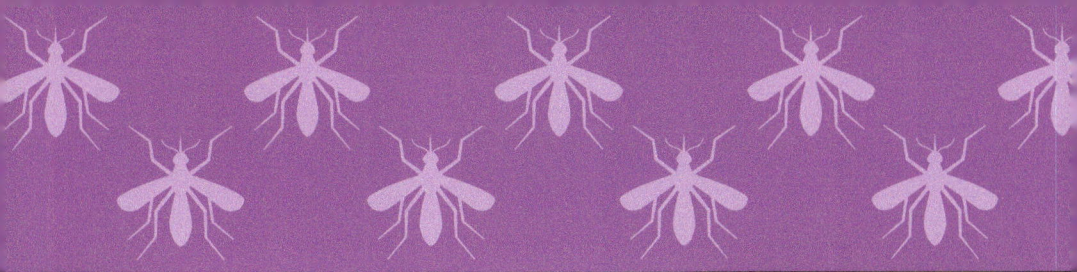

11

What Do Mosquitoes Eat?

All mosquitoes drink flower nectar and fruit juices. Nectar is a sweet **liquid** made by flowers.

Key Word

Liquid: something like water that flows freely and is not solid.

Female mosquitoes drink blood from people and animals. Blood helps them make eggs.

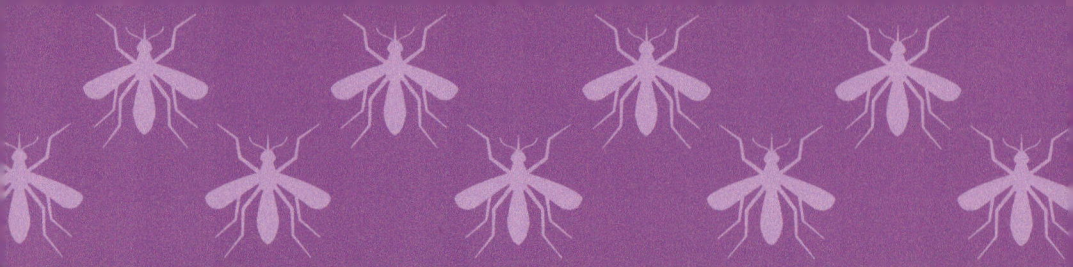

Female mosquitoes stick their straw-like mouth into the skin. This can leave a red, itchy mark.

Not all females drink blood. Some kinds of mosquitoes do not need it.

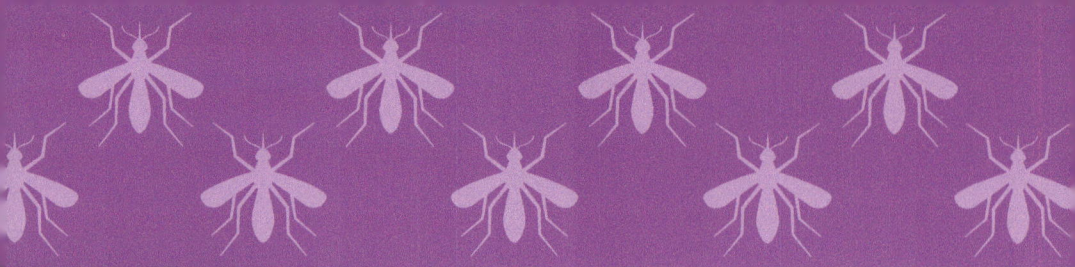

Mosquito Behavior

Mosquitoes like to eat from some people and animals more than others.

They are **attracted** to warmth. They are also attracted to dark colors.

Key Word

Attracted: strongly liking someone or something.

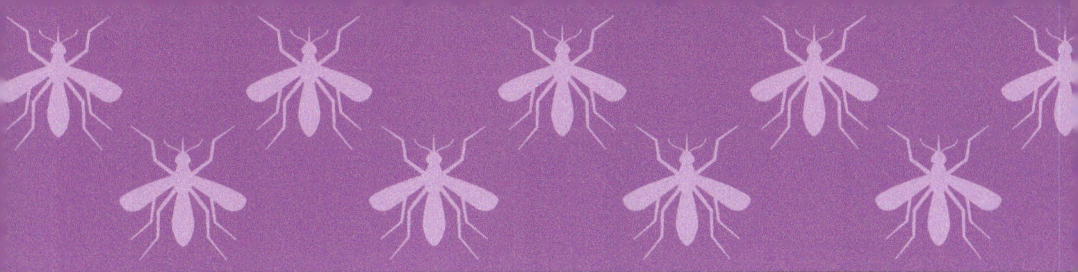

17

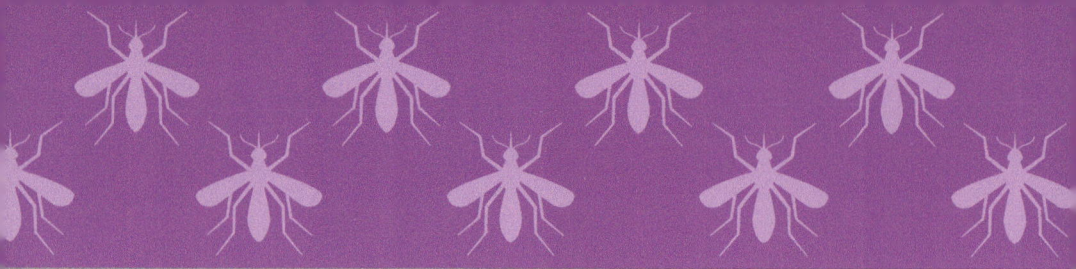

Mosquitoes are also attracted to carbon dioxide. This is the gas people breathe out.

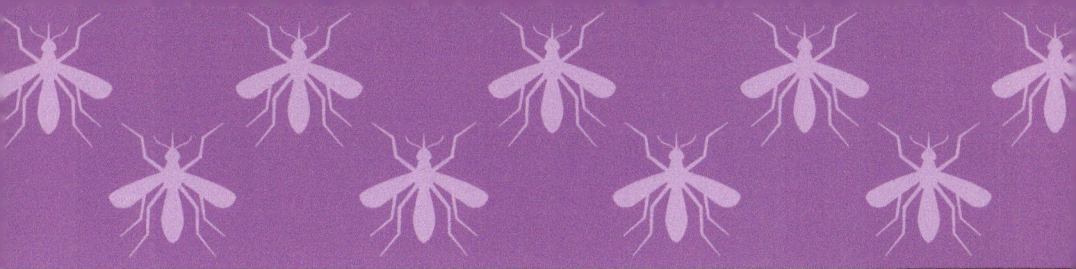

Sometimes the smell of someone's skin can attract mosquitoes. Some scientists think they like smelly feet.

19

Mosquito Life Cycle

Mosquitoes lay eggs in or near water. They are hard to find. They look just like dirt.

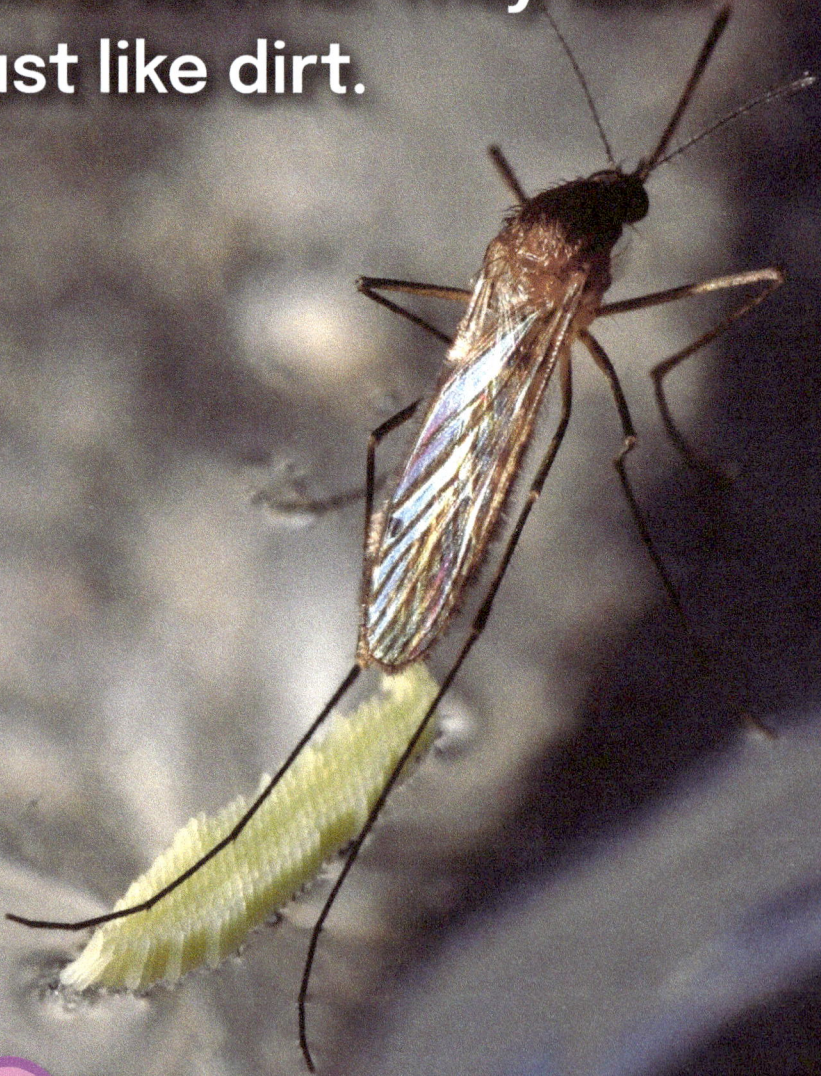

Eggs hatch into baby
mosquitoes called larvae.
Larvae turn into older
mosquitoes called pupae.

Larvae and pupae live in water. Shedding their skin helps both larvae and pupae grow.

Pupae become adults in two to seven days. Adult mosquitoes live for two to four weeks.

Fun Facts

Male mosquitoes find females by listening for the sound of their wings flapping.

Mosquitoes are more active when the moon is full.

Mosquitoes can flap their wings about 800 times in one second.

Male mosquitoes dance in groups to attract females.

Are Mosquitoes Helpful or Harmful?

Mosquitoes can be helpful. They are food for a lot of animals like birds and spiders.

Some mosquitoes are harmful. They carry **diseases**. Their bite can make people sick.

Key Word

Diseases: things that harm the health of people, animals, and plants.

27

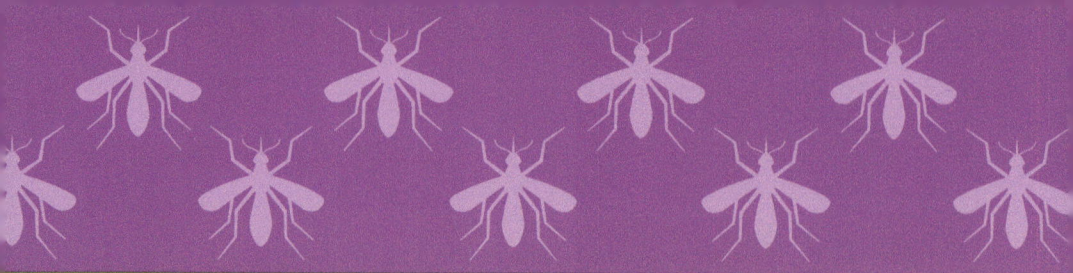

Are Mosquitoes in Danger?

Some animals are dying out. Mosquitoes are not one of them.

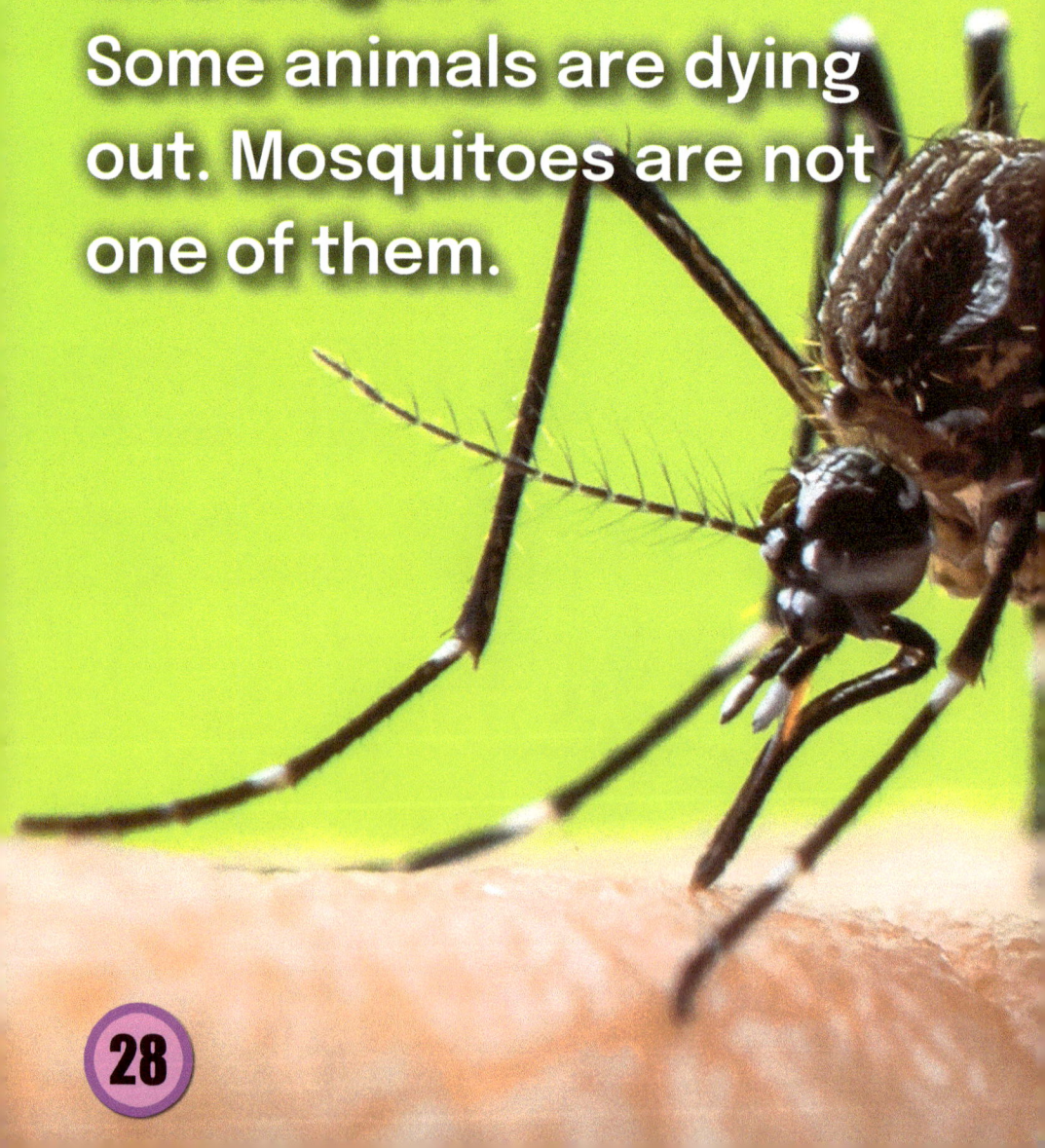

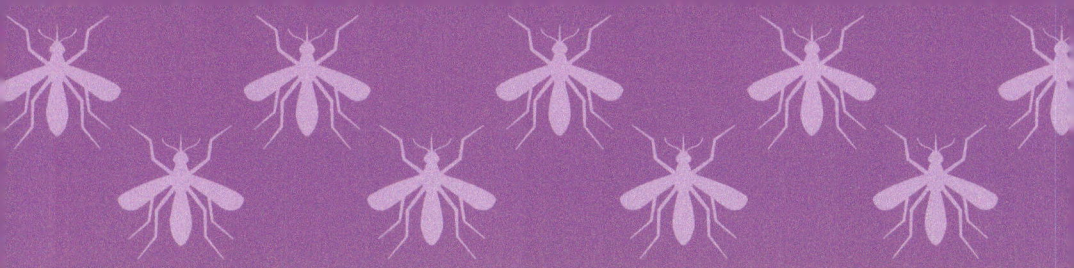

Mosquitoes are spreading to new places as the planet warms up. This helps them make more mosquitoes.

Quiz

Test your knowledge of mosquitoes by answering the following questions. The questions are based on what you have read in this book. The answers are listed on the bottom of the next page.

1 Are mosquitoes small flies?

2 Do mosquitoes live in Antarctica?

3 Do all females drink blood?

4 Are mosquito eggs hard to find?

5 Are mosquitoes more active when the moon is full?

6 Are some mosquitoes harmful?

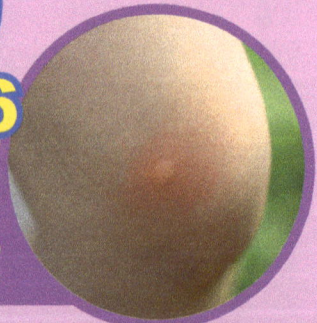

Explore other books in the
Backyard Bugs & Creepy Crawlies series!

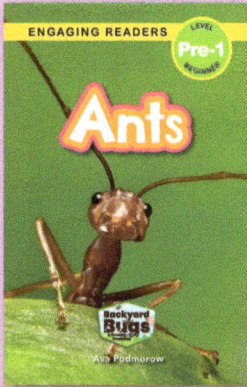

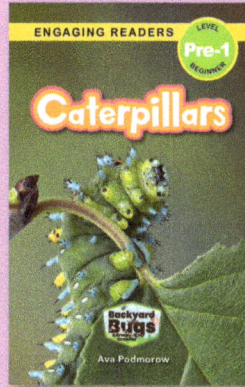

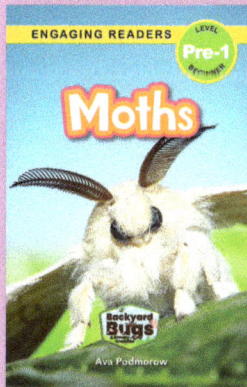

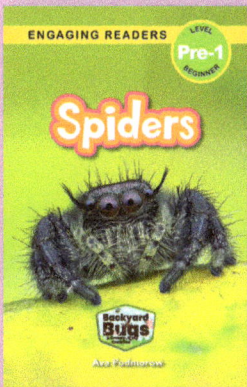

ENGAGING READERS — LEVEL Pre-1 BEGINNER

Ants
Backyard Bugs
Ava Podmorow

ENGAGING READERS — LEVEL Pre-1 BEGINNER

Beetles
Backyard Bugs
Victoria Hazlehurst

ENGAGING READERS — LEVEL Pre-1 BEGINNER

Caterpillars
Backyard Bugs
Ava Podmorow

ENGAGING READERS — LEVEL Pre-1 BEGINNER

Grasshoppers
Backyard Bugs
Ava Podmorow

ENGAGING READERS — LEVEL Pre-1 BEGINNER

Moths
Backyard Bugs
Ava Podmorow

ENGAGING READERS — LEVEL Pre-1 BEGINNER

Snails
Backyard Bugs
Ava Podmorow

ENGAGING READERS — LEVEL Pre-1 BEGINNER

Spiders
Backyard Bugs
Ava Podmorow

ENGAGING READERS — LEVEL Pre-1 BEGINNER

Wasps
Backyard Bugs
Sarah Harvey

ENGAGING READERS — LEVEL Pre-1 BEGINNER

Worms
Backyard Bugs
Victoria Hazlehurst

Visit www.engagebooks.com to explore more Engaging Readers.

Answers: 1. Yes 2. No 3. No 4. Yes 5. Yes 6. Yes

www.ingramcontent.com/pod-product-compliance
Lightning Source LLC
Chambersburg PA
CBHW052036030426

42337CB00027B/5026

* 9 7 8 1 7 7 8 7 8 7 1 5 7 *